Digital Fortress: Your Essential Guide to Online Security

Author: Markus Bergthaler

1

Table of Contents

About the Author

Markus Bergthaler is a cybersecurity and fraud prevention expert with extensive experience investigating financial crimes, online fraud, and cyber threats. Over the years, he has collaborated with the FBI, Interpol, and the Secret Service, working on high-profile fraud cases that have helped dismantle international criminal networks.

His expertise extends to anti-money laundering (AML), identity theft prevention, and social engineering tactics, as well as investigations into human trafficking rings that leverage financial fraud to operate in the shadows.

With a deep understanding of digital security, financial crime, and cyber investigations, Markus wrote *Digital Fortress: Your Essential Guide to Online Security* to equip everyday users with the tools to protect their digital lives. Through *Digital Fortress*, he demystifies cybersecurity, offering practical, easy-to-implement strategies to shield readers from hackers, scammers, and emerging threats.

Introduction

Welcome to *Digital Fortress: Your Essential Guide to Online Security*. In today's rapidly evolving digital landscape, our lives are more connected than ever before. From online shopping and banking to staying in touch with friends and managing work, almost every aspect of our daily routines depends on the internet. But with this convenience comes risk. Cyber threats, scams, and identity theft are not distant problems—they can affect anyone, at any time. This book is here to empower you with the knowledge and practical tools to protect yourself and your personal information in the digital world.

You might feel overwhelmed by headlines about massive data breaches—like those at Walmart, Ticketmaster, and T-Mobile in 2023, where millions of records were exposed—or sophisticated phishing scams, but you don't need to be a tech expert to defend against these threats. Whether you're a casual internet user or someone who manages sensitive information daily, the strategies outlined in this guide are designed to be accessible and effective. We break down complex topics like password security, two-factor authentication, and safe browsing practices into simple, actionable steps that you can implement right away.

Throughout this book, you'll discover the importance of establishing strong, unique passwords and learn how a password manager can simplify your digital life. You'll also explore the critical role of Multi-Factor Authentication (MFA)—including emerging biometric options like facial recognition—in adding an extra layer of protection to your accounts. With real-world examples, such as the Ticketmaster breach that compromised 560 million customers (TIME, 2024), and easy-to-follow instructions, you'll gain the confidence to recognize phishing attempts, use browser tools to spot fakes, and avoid scams that prey on unsuspecting users.

But digital security isn't just about protecting your online accounts. It's also about safeguarding your devices—from smartphones and laptops to tablets and desktops. We discuss essential practices like keeping software up-to-date, using antivirus programs, encrypting sensitive data, and ensuring physical security to prevent theft. In addition, we cover the safe use of public Wi-Fi, the benefits of Virtual Private Networks (VPNs)—including free options with caveats—and even future trends like blockchain for secure transactions, all to keep your internet connection safe when you're on the go.

By the end of this book, you will have built a robust foundation in digital security—a personal blueprint for staying safe online. Our goal is to transform what might seem like daunting technical jargon into clear, practical advice that fits seamlessly into your everyday routine, complete with checklists for quick action if you're hacked. Whether you're protecting your financial information, ensuring your social media privacy, managing third-party app risks, or simply browsing the web, every step you take adds another layer to your personal digital fortress. We also encourage you to stay informed as threats evolve and explore visual aids online to deepen your understanding.

So, take a deep breath and prepare to embark on a journey that will not only safeguard your data but also enhance your confidence in navigating the online world. Let's begin building your digital fortress—one secure step at a time.

Chapter 1: The Digital Age and the Need for Security

Picture yourself at a café, savoring a latte, scrolling through your phone when—ding!—an alert flashes: "Account Compromised!" You jostle your cup, splash a little coffee, and realize trouble's just tapped you on the shoulder. That's life in our connected world—a place where convenience is everywhere, but cybercriminals are the uninvited guests who keep showing up. The internet's woven into our daily lives, from banking to shopping to catching up with friends, yet it's also a hunting ground for those eager to nab your personal info.

We're all digital dabblers now—paying bills with a tap, ordering groceries online, sharing snippets of our lives with a click. It's a marvel, sure, but here's the rub: those handy tools also leave us open to some sneaky risks. Hackers don't care if you're a corporate hotshot or just someone who enjoys a good cat video—they'll take whatever they can snag. Got an email account? A social media profile? Ever used a credit card online? Then you're on their radar—no VIP status required.

Think cyber threats only chase the big fish? Nope. You're not just background noise—you're a target worth pursuing. This chapter's your kickoff: why cybersecurity's a must for everyone, what dangers are lurking, and how to start building your defenses without needing a tech wizard's handbook. We'll dive into the risks, spotlight the troublemakers, and get you ready to stay ahead—because in this digital game, a little smarts beats a lot of "oops" moments.

The Growing Cyber Threat Landscape: Trouble's Booming

Cybercrime's not some petty side gig—it's a full-blown operation, and the stats back it up. In 2023, over 4.5 billion records got scooped up, enough to give every person on Earth a cameo in a hacker's scrapbook. Even the heavyweights—Walmart, Ticketmaster, T-Mobile—couldn't dodge the hits. Walmart's Spark Driver portal sprung a leak, spilling Social Security numbers and driver's licenses after months of unauthorized poking around (Cybersecurity For Me, 2025). Ticketmaster's breach saw hackers grab details from 560 million customers—a haul so big it could clog a hard drive (TIME, 2024; Qohash, 2024). T-Mobile got slammed twice—37 million accounts in one go, then 836 more later, losing names, emails, and SSNs like they were handing out free samples (Dark Reading, 2023; Security Magazine, 2023).

These aren't rare blips—they're loud warnings. Hackers have ditched the amateur hour for pro-level moves, wielding tools that crack passwords faster than you can say "uh-oh," sending emails so polished you'd think they're from your bank's PR team, and locking files with ransomware until you pay up—often in cryptocurrency, because even crooks like a modern twist. The FBI's Internet Crime Complaint Center clocked $12.5 billion in losses in 2023, up 22% from the year before. That's not spare change—that's a hefty pile of cash.

It's not just the big names, either. Capital One's 2019 slip let a single hacker, Paige Thompson, nab 100 million customers' data—credit scores, SSNs, the lot—because someone left a server wide open. No fancy tricks, just a gap she strolled through. Marriott's 2018 flub saw

500 million guests' details leak over years—passport numbers included—because they didn't lock down a database from a merger. And back in 2013, Yahoo handed over 3 billion accounts' worth of info—no encryption, just a whoopsie. These slip-ups, from giants to small fries, show the mess isn't occasional—it's a constant hum.

The scope keeps swelling. Every new gadget, app, or account adds another thread to the web hackers spin. That online store you shopped at once? Could leak your email tomorrow. The fitness app tracking your steps? Might be next. It's not about living scared—it's about knowing why a little caution goes a long way.

Why Do Cybercriminals Target Everyday People? You're the Easy Win

Forget the "I'm too small" excuse—you're a target because you're worth it, plain and simple. Hackers don't need you to be a mogul; they just need you to be human. Companies might have IT teams and sturdy defenses, but most of us don't, and that's their opening. Here's why you're in their sights:

- **Easy-to-Guess Passwords** – Verizon's 2023 Data Breach Report ties 81% of breaches to weak or stolen passwords. "123456" collapses quicker than a paper umbrella, and "Qwerty" might as well wave a white flag. Reuse those across sites, and one crack unlocks your whole life.

- **Lack of Awareness** – Businesses drill scam-spotting into staff; most folks just wing it with a "that looks odd" hunch. Ever clicked a "Package Delayed!" email half-distracted? That's their moment—they know you're not always on high alert.

- **Valuable Personal Info** – Your name, birthdate, and address might seem humdrum, but on the dark web, they're a few bucks each. Add an SSN, and it's a bonanza.

Share your dog's name online? That's a security question begging to be sniffed out.

- **Unsecured Devices and Networks** – That free Wi-Fi at the mall? A hacker's picnic. Using an old phone because "it still works"? An open door. No antivirus? You're rolling out the welcome mat.

Real life paints the picture. Take John from Ohio—he used "John1985" everywhere. A gaming site breach in 2022 spilled it, and hackers hit his PayPal, email, and eBay, racking up $2,000 in charges while he stared at his drained account. Or my pal who clicked a "free gift" link on social media—she handed over her login, and soon her friends got "I'm broke, help!" messages from "her." These aren't wild tales; they're everyday wake-ups showing why you're worth the effort.

It's not just lone wolves, either. Families get hit—my cousin posted her kids' birthdays online, and a scammer used it to guess her banking security questions, draining $500 before she caught on. Small businesses aren't safe—think of the local shop that skips updates, only to find customer emails leaked. You're not a nobody; you're a link in a chain they're eager to tug.

Common Online Threats: The Usual Culprits

So, who's behind the curtain? Let's meet the lineup—troublemakers with more moves than a chess grandmaster.

Phishing Attacks: The Sneaky Hook

Phishing's the classic play—simple, sharp, and all too common. You get an email from "Your Bank" shouting, "Your account's in trouble—click here!" It looks real, so you click, landing on a fake site that snags your login. The Anti-Phishing Working Group tracked 1.2 million attacks in 2023, up 15% from the year prior. I got a "FedEx" text about a "lost package"—"delivery" instead of "delivery" gave it away, but plenty don't spot the slip. Verizon says 36% of breaches start here—check senders (like "paypal.com" with a tricky "I"), hover over links, and lean on MFA to block them cold.

A coworker fell for an "Amazon account locked!" text—spot-on branding, but the link hit "amaz0n.co." He clicked, lost his creds, and hackers ordered a $300 gadget. A quick sender peek could've saved him—don't let a rushed moment cost you.

Data Breaches: Companies' Big Oops

Data breaches are when firms fumble—handing hackers your info like it's a free sample. Yahoo's 2013 breach lost 3 billion accounts' data—no encryption, just a shrug. Users reusing "YahooFan" got burned everywhere. Marriott's 2018 slip let 500 million guests' details leak over years—passport numbers included—because they didn't secure a merged system. Ticketmaster's 2023 hit saw folks who didn't swap passwords find their Spotify playing tunes they'd never pick—hackers have rotten taste. Unique passwords and haveibeenpwned.com are your shield—check if you're out there.

My neighbor ignored Marriott's alert, reused her password, and lost $1,000 to a mystery charge. A breach check could've spared her—your info's likely floating around too. Even small leaks—like a local retailer's customer list—can sting.

Identity Theft: Your Life, Their Party

Identity theft's when hackers take your info and live it up—new cards, loans, maybe a speeding ticket in your name. The FTC logged 1.1 million cases in 2023, fueled by breaches and oversharing. One woman posted her driver's license online—new ID flex—and hackers opened a $10,000 credit line while she basked in likes. Freeze your credit (free at Experian, Equifax, TransUnion), use MFA, and skip sharing your kid's birthdate—little Sophie doesn't need the fame.

A friend's sister shared her passport pic on social media—next thing, she's fighting fake debts. Months of hassle later, she wished she'd locked her credit. It's not overthinking—it's outsmarting.

Social Engineering: The Trust Trap

Social engineering's the human hook—tricking you, not your tech. Imagine a call from "Microsoft" saying, "Your PC's infected—let us in!" In 2021, a scammer posing as a bank rep talked a man out of $25,000 with a "verification" tale. Or the "Grandma, I'm in jail!" text—panic's their ace. I got a "Windows license expired" call—on my Mac, no less. Hang up, call legit numbers, and don't buy the sob story—the FBI says 70% of scams lean on this.

My aunt nearly sent $200 to a "tech support" caller claiming her ancient PC was a virus hub—she almost bit until I stepped in. A quick "no way" saved her—doubt's your best buddy.

Final Thoughts: Your Digital Starting Line

Our connected world's a wonder—convenience at every turn—but it's got a shadow side. Cybersecurity's not a luxury unless you're okay with hackers hosting a bash with your life. Walmart,

Ticketmaster, Capital One—they're proof the threat's real, and Marriott, Yahoo, and others show it's been humming along for years. But here's the bright spot: you don't need a tech degree to stay safe. Solid passwords, a bit of "hold on a sec," and the steps we'll unpack next can turn you from an easy mark to a tough nut.

Up next, we'll dive into password know-how that'll stump the bad guys, scam-spotting tricks to keep you sharp, and a plan to lock down your digital life. You'll breeze through online chaos with a knowing nod—ready to take the reins? Let's keep going.

Chapter 2: Password Security – Your First Line of Defense

Your password stands as the gatekeeper to your digital world—a weak one's like leaving your front door wide open, practically begging hackers to drop by. It's your first, and most essential, shield against cybercriminals, yet countless folks still use passwords so flimsy they'd lose a tug-of-war with a toddler. That's a risky bet, because today's hackers wield tools that can crack codes faster than you can misplace your keys.

You might think, "Nobody's after my stuff—I'm small potatoes." Not quite. If a hacker grabs your email password, they can reset your bank logins, hijack your social media, and turn your online life into a mess. One shaky password can spiral into identity theft, drained accounts, or your friends getting weird messages from "you." This chapter's your roadmap to building passwords that hold strong, dodging the reuse trap, and letting a password manager make it all feel like a breeze.

Why Weak Passwords Are a Hacker's Dream

Hackers don't guess passwords one-by-one in some dimly lit basement—they've got automated software that blasts through millions of combinations in seconds. Verizon's 2023 Data Breach Investigations Report tied 81% of breaches to weak or stolen passwords—a glaring sign of trouble. Here's why common missteps leave you exposed:

- **Simple Passwords** – "123456" or "password" might feel cozy, but they're cracked faster than a cheap lock.

SplashData's 2023 list pegged "123456" as the top flop—used by millions, broken in a blink.

- **Personal Tidbits** – Name, birthdate, or pet's name in there? Hackers can scoop that from your social media faster than you can post "Happy Birthday, Rover!" "Rover2020" isn't sneaky—it's bait.
- **Reusing Passwords** – One password leaked in a breach gets tested everywhere—credential stuffing's their play. A single slip, and your digital life's up for grabs.
- **Short Passwords** – Six characters? Done in a snap. Twelve with letters, numbers, and symbols? That's a fortress—centuries of hacking time to bust.

The 2023 Ticketmaster breach hit 560 million accounts (TIME, 2024)—folks reusing "TicketFan1" saw hackers raid their Spotify, email, even banks. Weak passwords don't just flirt with danger—they throw the door wide open.

Building Passwords That Stand Tall

A strong password isn't optional—it's your digital backbone. Here's what makes it tough:

- **Length** – Aim for 12-16 characters. Short ones are appetizers; long ones are a meal hackers can't swallow.
- **Mix It Up** – Uppercase, lowercase, numbers, symbols—like a recipe with all the trimmings. "P@ssw0rd" fails; "Gr33n!Tiger$22" holds firm.
- **Uniqueness** – Every account gets its own. Reusing is like handing out spare keys to every lock you've got—one lost, all gone.
- **Memorable but Random** – Easy for you, nonsense to them. Forget "John1980"—go for "Blue!Rain$Forest9."

Why sweat it? NordPass's 2023 study clocked "password" at 0.1 seconds to crack; "G7v!kP$mQz9xL2" at over a billion years. That's a time gap you can lean on—math's your pal here.

Passwords You Won't Forget

Random strings like "X7kP!m9Qz" are a bear—to crack and to remember. Passphrases save the day: word combos that stick with you but stump hackers. "Green!Tiger$Jumps22" paints a picture—a tiger bounding through a forest—while keeping it rock-solid. Compare that to "Mypassword1!"—a pushover that caves in a flash.

In 2022, a guy lost $5,000 reusing "Love2020" across accounts—a sweet nod to his wife that hackers turned bitter, draining his PayPal (Forbes, 2022). A passphrase like "Sunny!Hill$Bikes44" would've kept his cash safe and his heart intact. It's strength with a side of sanity—your brain will thank you.

Switching to Strong Passwords

Got a mess of weak passwords? Don't panic—swap them out step-by-step. Kick off with your email—it's the skeleton key to your online life. The 2023 Ticketmaster breach (TIME, 2024) showed the stakes: 560 million accounts hit, and folks reusing passwords lost big across the board. Change your email first, then banking, then social media—one lock at a time builds the wall.

A password manager's your shortcut, spitting out winners like "R3d!Cloud$Flys77." My neighbor ignored this after a breach—stuck with "Summer22" everywhere—and saw $800 vanish to a hacker's shopping spree. Start with your VIP accounts—each new password's a brick in your digital defenses.

The Password Manager Lifeline

Keeping track of dozens of 16-character passwords is a brain-bender—unless you've got a password manager. It generates, stores, and autofills strong passwords, leaving you with one master key to remember. After T-Mobile's 2023 breach exposed 37 million accounts (Dark Reading, 2023), manager users brushed it off—others were left scrambling to reset everything.

Top choices include:

- **1Password** – Secure, simple, great for families.
- **ProtonPass** – Privacy-first, locked up tight.
- **iCloud Keychain** – Free for Apple fans, syncs across gadgets.

My uncle swore by scribbled notes—until his cat knocked them off the desk, and he lost Netflix to a "helpful" cousin. One master password beats a shredded pile—give it a try, and you'll wonder why you ever scribbled.

Steering Clear of Password Traps

Even strong passwords stumble if you trip here:

- **No Sticky Notes** – "P@ssw0rd123" on your monitor? A hacker's selfie away from payday—keep it digital, not dangling.
- **Don't Share** – Need to lend access? Use a manager's sharing tool, not a text. My pal emailed "DogLover99" to his brother—brother's inbox got hacked, and so did he.
- **Tricky Security Questions** – "Mom's maiden name" as "Smith"? Too easy. Try "!BlueTiger$45"—make it a mini-password.

In 2023, a phishing wave nabbed security answers from overshared social media—birthdates and pet names were hacker candy. Lock those answers tight—treat them like gold.

Your Password Game Plan

Your passwords are your digital lifeline—weak ones leave you hanging; strong ones keep you steady. Breaches like Walmart's (Cybersecurity For Me, 2025) and T-Mobile's (Dark Reading, 2023) drove it home—37 million accounts exposed showed how fast flimsy passwords flop. Strong, unique passwords, a manager to tame them, and MFA (up next) turn your accounts into a no-go zone for hackers.

Key Takeaways:

- Go long and strong—12-16 characters, all mixed up.
- Never reuse—each account's its own puzzle.
- Grab a password manager—1Password or ProtonPass are your pals.
- Add MFA—Chapter 3's got the scoop.

Ready to bolt that gate? Let's stack on another layer of protection next.

Chapter 3: Multi-Factor Authentication (MFA) – Your Extra Security Shield

Even the strongest passwords can be compromised. That's where Multi-Factor Authentication (MFA) comes in.

MFA adds an extra layer of security to your accounts by requiring not just a password but a second form of verification. This means that even if a hacker manages to steal your password, they won't be able to access your account without the second authentication factor.

Why Passwords Alone Aren't Enough

Cybercriminals have become highly efficient at stealing passwords through:

- Phishing attacks that trick you into entering credentials on fake websites
- Data breaches that leak login information onto the dark web
- Keyloggers and malware that record your keystrokes

Since many people reuse passwords, hackers can use stolen credentials to break into multiple accounts in what's known as a credential stuffing attack. This is why having a second layer of protection like MFA is crucial.

How MFA Works

When you enable Multi-Factor Authentication, logging into an account requires:

- Your password (something you know)
- A second authentication factor (something you have or something you are)

This second factor could be:

- A one-time code from an authenticator app (e.g., Google Authenticator, Authy)
- A physical security key like YubiKey or Titan Key
- A biometric scan (fingerprint or facial recognition)

Without access to this second authentication factor, a hacker cannot access your account—even if they have your password.

Types of Multi-Factor Authentication (Ranked by Security Level)

Not all MFA methods are equally secure. Here's how they compare:

- **Weakest: SMS-Based MFA** – Sends a one-time code via text message. Vulnerable to SIM-swapping attacks (hackers can hijack your phone number).
- **More Secure: Authenticator Apps** – Generates a temporary, time-based code in an app like Google Authenticator or Authy. Not vulnerable to SIM-swaps because it's app-based.
- **Most Secure: Hardware Security Keys** – Physical device (YubiKey, Titan Key) required for login. Virtually impossible to hack remotely. Used by security-conscious organizations like Google, Microsoft, and banks.

For everyday users, an authenticator app is a good balance between security and convenience. However, if you're dealing with highly sensitive accounts (banking, business accounts, or cryptocurrency wallets), consider using a hardware security key.

Emerging MFA Technologies

Looking into the future, biometric MFA—like facial recognition or voice authentication—might become more common, offering an even more secure and seamless method of verification. These technologies rely on unique physical traits, making them harder to replicate than traditional methods, though they require careful implementation to protect privacy and prevent spoofing.

How to Enable MFA on Your Accounts

Setting up Multi-Factor Authentication is simple:

- Go to your account's security settings (Google, Facebook, banking apps, etc.).
- Look for "Multi-Factor Authentication" or "Two-Factor Authentication."
- Choose your preferred method:

Use an authenticator app (Google Authenticator, Authy) for better security.

Avoid using SMS-based MFA unless no other option is available.

- Save your backup codes in case you lose access to your device.
- Use a hardware security key if your account supports it.

Pro Tip: Prioritize enabling MFA on your most critical accounts first:

- Email accounts (Gmail, Outlook) – Your email is the gateway to all your accounts.
- Banking & financial services – Prevent unauthorized access to your money.
- Social media – Avoid account takeovers and impersonation scams.
- Online shopping & subscriptions – Prevent fraudulent purchases.

What If You Lose Your MFA Device?

Losing your phone or security key can be frustrating, but don't panic:

- Use backup codes – Most services give you backup codes when setting up MFA. Store these safely!
- Use a backup MFA method – Some services allow you to register multiple MFA devices.
- Contact support – If all else fails, reach out to the platform's support team to regain access.

Avoid storing backup codes in your email—instead, keep them in a secure notes app or your password manager.

Final Thoughts on Multi-Factor Authentication

MFA is one of the simplest and most effective ways to protect your accounts. Avoid SMS-based MFA if possible—use an authenticator app or security key instead. Prioritize enabling MFA on your most important accounts first. With emerging biometric technologies on the horizon, MFA continues to evolve, offering even greater protection. By taking a few extra seconds to authenticate your logins, you're making it exponentially harder for hackers to access your accounts.

Chapter 4: Safe Browsing and Avoiding Scams

The internet is a powerful tool, but it's also filled with traps, scams, and malicious actors waiting to take advantage of unsuspecting users. Cybercriminals use sophisticated tactics to trick people into revealing personal information, installing malware, or falling for fraudulent schemes.

In this chapter, we'll cover how to browse the internet safely, identify scams, and protect yourself from online fraud.

Recognizing and Avoiding Phishing Scams

Phishing scams are one of the most common online threats. Cybercriminals send emails, text messages, or create fake websites designed to trick you into entering your login credentials or personal data.

How Phishing Works:

- A scammer sends a fake email pretending to be from a trusted company (e.g., your bank, PayPal, Amazon).
- The email contains an urgent request, like "Your account has been compromised. Click here to reset your password."
- The link directs you to a fake website that looks legitimate but is designed to steal your information.
- Once you enter your login details, the hacker gains access to your account.

How to Spot a Phishing Email:

- Look for misspellings and grammatical errors – Legitimate companies have professional communication.

- Check the sender's email address – A fake email may come from instead of .
- Hover over links before clicking – The URL should match the company's official website.
- Be wary of urgent requests – Scammers create a sense of urgency to pressure you into acting quickly.

How to Protect Yourself:

- Never click on suspicious links in emails or text messages.
- Always visit websites by typing the official URL into your browser instead of clicking links.
- Enable Multi-Factor Authentication (MFA) to prevent hackers from accessing your account even if they steal your password.

Using Browser Tools to Detect Phishing

For the tech-savvy, using browser developer tools can help you inspect links before clicking. Right-click on a link, select "Inspect" or "View Source," and look for any suspicious redirects or scripts. If the URL doesn't match the company's official domain or contains unexpected code, it's likely a phishing attempt.

Malicious Websites: How to Browse Safely

Many websites contain malware, fake advertisements, or scams designed to exploit visitors. Here's how to ensure a safe browsing experience:

- Look for HTTPS – Secure websites use HTTPS (instead of HTTP) and display a padlock icon in the browser address bar.

- Use a reputable web browser – Browsers like Chrome, Firefox, and Edge include built-in security features that warn you about malicious websites.

- Install browser security extensions – Tools like uBlock Origin, Privacy Badger, or HTTPS Everywhere can block harmful content.

- Never download software from unfamiliar sites – Download programs only from official websites or app stores.

Common Online Scams and How to Avoid Them

Cybercriminals use different scams to target victims online. Here are some of the most common scams and how to protect yourself:

Tech Support Scams

- A pop-up appears on your screen saying, "Your computer has been infected! Call this number for assistance."

- The scammer pretends to be Microsoft or Apple support, convincing you to grant them remote access to your computer.

- They install malware or demand payment for fake repairs.

How to Avoid It:

- Legitimate companies will never display pop-up warnings or ask you to call them.

- If you suspect an issue, contact the company directly through their official website.

- Never allow remote access to your computer unless you initiated the support request.

Fake E-Commerce Websites

- You find an amazing deal on a brand-name product— often too good to be true.

- The website looks professional but has no customer reviews or contact information.
- You place an order but never receive the product—or worse, your credit card is stolen.

How to Avoid It:

- Shop only from reputable websites (Amazon, Best Buy, official brand stores).
- Verify seller ratings and reviews before making a purchase.
- Use a virtual credit card or PayPal for extra security.

Lottery and Giveaway Scams

- You receive an email saying, "Congratulations! You've won a $1,000 gift card!"
- To claim your prize, you must provide personal information or pay a small fee.
- Once you comply, you get nothing—and your data is stolen.

How to Avoid It:

- If you didn't enter a contest, you didn't win anything.
- Legitimate giveaways don't ask for payments or personal details upfront.
- Ignore and delete suspicious emails or messages.

Safe Online Shopping Practices

With online shopping becoming more common, it's essential to follow these best practices to avoid fraud and identity theft:

- Only shop on secure websites – Stick to well-known retailers and verify a site's legitimacy before entering payment information.

- Use a virtual credit card – Many banks and services like PayPal offer virtual cards that generate a temporary card number to prevent fraud.
- Beware of fake discounts – Scammers create fake online stores that mimic real brands, offering massive discounts to lure victims.

Using a VPN for Extra Protection

A VPN (Virtual Private Network) adds another layer of security when browsing online, especially on public Wi-Fi.

- Encrypts your internet traffic, preventing hackers from intercepting data.
- Hides your IP address, making it harder for advertisers and cybercriminals to track you.
- Lets you securely access content when traveling by masking your location.

Popular VPNs include: NordVPN, ExpressVPN, and ProtonVPN.

Tip: If you often use public Wi-Fi at cafes, airports, or hotels, a VPN is a must-have.

Final Thoughts on Safe Browsing and Scam Prevention

Think before you click – Phishing scams are everywhere, so always verify links and emails. Use security tools – Browser extensions, antivirus software, and VPNs help keep you safe. Avoid giving out personal information – Scammers thrive on data, so be cautious about what you share online. Shop smart – Stick to reputable e-commerce sites and use secure payment methods. Leveraging tools like browser developer tools can give tech-savvy users an edge in spotting phishing attempts. By following these safe browsing habits, you'll drastically reduce your risk of online fraud and scams.

Chapter 5: Protecting Your Devices and Data

Your personal devices—smartphones, tablets, laptops, and desktops—are the gateways to your entire digital life. If compromised, a hacker can access your emails, financial accounts, private messages, and sensitive files. Keeping your devices secure is just as important as having strong passwords or using Multi-Factor Authentication (MFA).

In this chapter, you'll learn how to secure your devices, prevent malware infections, and protect your personal data from cyber threats.

Keeping Your Software and Operating System Updated

One of the biggest vulnerabilities in cybersecurity is outdated software. Cybercriminals often exploit security flaws in operating systems and applications before companies can patch them.

Why updates matter:

- Security patches fix vulnerabilities that hackers exploit.
- Updates often include performance improvements and bug fixes.
- Cybercriminals target users who don't update their software, using automated tools to scan for weaknesses.

How to stay updated:

- Enable automatic updates for your operating system (Windows, macOS, iOS, Android).
- Keep apps, browsers, and antivirus software up to date.
- Update firmware for routers, smart devices, and Internet of Things (IoT) devices.

Tip: If a device or software no longer receives security updates, it's time to replace it. Using unsupported software (like old Windows versions) exposes you to high-risk vulnerabilities.

Using Antivirus and Anti-Malware Protection

No matter how cautious you are, malware (viruses, ransomware, spyware) can still find its way onto your device. Antivirus software serves as a critical line of defense against these threats.

How malware spreads:

- Email attachments and phishing links
- Fake software downloads from shady websites
- Malicious ads (malvertising) on compromised websites
- Infected USB drives or external storage

How to protect yourself:

- Install a reputable antivirus program (Bitdefender, Malwarebytes, Norton).
- Run regular scans to check for threats.
- Enable real-time protection to block malware before it executes.
- Never download software from untrusted sources.

Pro Tip: Combine traditional antivirus with anti-malware software like Malwarebytes for additional security.

Enabling Encryption for Sensitive Data

Encryption protects your files, emails, and messages by scrambling data so that only authorized users can access it. If your device is stolen or hacked, encrypted files remain secure.

How to encrypt your devices:

- Windows: Enable BitLocker (found in Control Panel > System & Security).
- Mac: Use FileVault (System Preferences > Security & Privacy).
- iPhones & Android Phones: Enable built-in encryption (found in security settings).

Tip: Always use strong passwords with encryption tools for maximum security.

Securing Your Smartphone: The Most Valuable Target for Hackers

Your smartphone is often more valuable than your laptop—it contains banking apps, saved passwords, private messages, and even biometric data. Protect it like you would your wallet!

How to secure your phone:

- Use a strong PIN, password, or biometric lock (fingerprint/Face ID).
- Enable remote tracking & wiping (Find My iPhone, Google Find My Device).
- Disable Bluetooth and Wi-Fi when not in use to avoid unauthorized connections.
- Never install apps from outside the official App Store or Google Play Store.

Beware of SIM Swapping! Hackers can social-engineer their way into stealing your phone number from your carrier. Once they have control of your number, they can bypass SMS-based Multi-Factor Authentication (MFA) and take over your accounts.

How to prevent SIM Swapping:

- Contact your mobile carrier and set up a PIN or password for your account.
- Use an authenticator app for MFA instead of SMS-based codes.

Physical Security of Devices

Physical security matters too. Always keep your devices in sight or locked away when in public to prevent theft or unauthorized access. A stolen device without a strong lock or encryption can give attackers immediate access to your digital life.

Backing Up Your Data: The Ultimate Safety Net

Even with top-tier security, things can go wrong. Devices fail, get stolen, or become infected with ransomware. A solid backup strategy ensures that you never lose important files.

Best backup practices:

- Use cloud storage (Google Drive, iCloud, OneDrive) for easy access.
- Create local backups on an external hard drive or NAS (Network-Attached Storage).
- Follow the 3-2-1 backup rule:

3 copies of your data

2 different storage types (cloud + external drive)

1 offsite backup (to protect against physical damage, fires, or theft).

Tip: Encrypt your backups to protect sensitive information in case of theft or hacking.

Final Thoughts on Device and Data Protection

Keep your software updated – Don't ignore security patches. Use antivirus and anti-malware software – Prevention is key. Encrypt your data – Protect against unauthorized access. Secure your smartphone – It's your most vulnerable device. Back up your data – Always have a recovery plan. Don't overlook physical security— keeping your devices physically safe is just as critical as protecting them from digital threats. By following these steps, your devices and data will be far more resilient against cyber threats.

Chapter 6: Securing Online Transactions and Financial Data

Online banking, shopping, and digital payments have made our lives more convenient, but they also come with significant security risks. Cybercriminals constantly look for ways to steal financial data, whether through phishing attacks, fake websites, data breaches, or malware.

In this chapter, we'll cover how to secure your financial transactions, protect your credit and debit cards, and prevent fraud when shopping online.

The Most Common Financial Threats

- Phishing Scams: Fake emails or messages pretending to be from your bank or a payment service, tricking you into revealing account details.
- Credit Card Skimming: Hidden card readers steal your payment information at ATMs or payment terminals.
- Fake E-Commerce Sites: Fraudulent websites that collect payments but never deliver products.
- Public Wi-Fi Eavesdropping: Hackers intercept financial transactions on unsecured networks.
- Account Takeover Fraud: Criminals gain access to your bank or payment accounts through leaked credentials or social engineering.

By recognizing these threats, you can take steps to secure your financial information before hackers exploit it.

How to Secure Your Online Transactions

1. Always Use Trusted and Secure Websites

- Look for HTTPS in the website address before entering any payment details.
- Stick to reputable retailers like Amazon, Best Buy, or official brand websites.
- Red Flag: A website offering expensive items at unrealistically low prices is likely a scam.

2. Use Virtual Credit Cards for Extra Protection

- Many banks and services like Revolut, Capital One, or PayPal offer virtual credit cards, which generate a temporary card number for online purchases.
- Benefits of Virtual Credit Cards:

The number expires after use, preventing fraudsters from reusing it.

It protects your real credit card from data breaches.

Some services let you set spending limits for extra control.

- If your bank offers virtual cards, use them for online purchases whenever possible.

3. Enable Fraud Alerts and Purchase Notifications

- Most banks and credit card providers let you turn on transaction alerts so you'll know immediately if there's suspicious activity on your account.
- Set up text or email alerts for transactions over a specific amount.
- Regularly review your bank and credit card statements for unfamiliar charges.
- Report any suspicious transactions to your bank immediately.
- If you see an unauthorized charge, report it ASAP—banks typically allow chargebacks for fraudulent transactions within a certain period.

4. Use Secure Payment Methods (Avoid Debit Cards Online!)

- Best Payment Methods for Security:

Credit Cards – Offer fraud protection and the ability to dispute unauthorized charges.

PayPal – Hides your payment details and provides an extra layer of protection.

Apple Pay / Google Pay – Use tokenized payments, meaning your real card number is never shared.

- Avoid Using:

Debit Cards – Less fraud protection than credit cards.

Wire Transfers (Western Union, MoneyGram) – Often used in scams; hard to recover lost money.

- Note: If a merchant only accepts wire transfers, it's a major red flag!

Blockchain Technology: A Future Trend

Looking ahead, blockchain technology promises to enhance transaction security by providing a decentralized ledger, reducing the risk of fraud. By recording transactions in an immutable, transparent way, blockchain could make financial data harder to tamper with, offering a potential game-changer for secure online payments.

Protecting Your Bank and Payment Accounts

1. Enable Multi-Factor Authentication (MFA) on Banking Apps

- Most banks and payment providers offer MFA, which prevents unauthorized logins.

- Use an authenticator app (not SMS-based MFA) for better security.
- If your bank supports biometric authentication (Face ID, fingerprint scanning), enable it.

2. Keep Your Banking Information Private

- Never share your banking details via email, text, or over the phone.
- Be wary of "urgent" calls claiming to be from your bank—banks don't ask for sensitive information over the phone.
- If you receive a suspicious banking email, go directly to your bank's website instead of clicking any links.
- If someone calls claiming to be from your bank and asks for personal information, hang up and call your bank's official number instead.

3. Keep Your Credit Reports Locked

- Cybercriminals often use stolen personal information to open fraudulent accounts in your name. Locking or freezing your credit prevents unauthorized loans or credit applications.
- How to Freeze Your Credit:

Contact the three major credit bureaus (Experian, Equifax, TransUnion) and request a credit freeze.

It's completely free and prevents anyone from opening a new credit account in your name.

You can unfreeze it temporarily when you need to apply for a loan or credit card.

- Tip: Freezing your credit does not affect your credit score. It simply prevents fraudsters from taking out loans in your name.

What to Do If Your Financial Information Is Compromised

1. Contact Your Bank Immediately

- Report unauthorized charges or suspicious activity to your bank or credit card issuer.
- Freeze or replace compromised cards before more damage is done.

2. Change Your Passwords & Secure Your Accounts

- Reset passwords for banking, email, and shopping accounts.
- Enable MFA on all financial accounts to prevent further breaches.

3. Monitor Your Credit Report for Fraud

- Use free credit monitoring services to check for unauthorized activity.
- If identity theft is suspected, file a fraud report with the FTC (in the U.S.) or your local fraud prevention agency.

Tip: If you've been hacked, notify your bank, credit bureaus, and law enforcement to document the incident.

Final Thoughts on Securing Financial Transactions

Always shop on trusted sites – Look for HTTPS and avoid suspicious retailers. Use virtual credit cards – Protect yourself against fraud and data breaches. Turn on bank alerts – Stay informed about unusual activity. Freeze your credit – Prevent identity theft and unauthorized loans. Use secure payment methods – Credit cards and PayPal offer better protection than debit cards. As blockchain technology emerges, it may further revolutionize how we secure transactions, adding another layer of defense. By following these financial security measures, you can protect your hard-earned money from cybercriminals and fraudsters.

Chapter 7: Social Media and Privacy Protection

Social media has transformed the way we connect with others, share our lives, and consume information. But as much as it enhances our daily interactions, it also exposes us to privacy risks, scams, and identity theft.

Cybercriminals, scammers, and even data-hungry corporations actively monitor social media to exploit personal details. Whether it's through social engineering attacks, hacked accounts, or oversharing private information, social media can be a security minefield.

In this chapter, you'll learn how to protect your social media accounts, safeguard your personal information, and avoid common social media scams.

The Risks of Oversharing on Social Media

Many people unknowingly give away too much personal information online. Even seemingly harmless details can be used by cybercriminals to impersonate you, steal your identity, or trick you into scams.

Common oversharing mistakes:

- Posting your full birthdate – Helps hackers guess passwords and security questions.
- "Checking in" at locations in real-time – Lets criminals know when your home is empty.
- Sharing vacation plans publicly – A goldmine for burglars looking for empty houses.

- Posting photos of sensitive documents (plane tickets, driver's licenses, vaccine cards) – Hackers can steal your personal data.

Example of a Social Media Fail: A woman once posted a selfie of her plane ticket before an international flight. Hackers used the barcode on the ticket to access her airline account, cancel her return flight, and steal her travel miles. Moral of the story: Never post boarding passes, ID cards, or credit cards!

How to share safely:

- Avoid posting personal details like your home address, phone number, or workplace.
- Set your profiles to private so only trusted people can see your posts.
- Wait until after your vacation to post travel pictures.

How to Secure Your Social Media Accounts

1. Use Strong, Unique Passwords for Every Platform

- Your social media accounts are prime targets for hackers. If someone gains access to your accounts, they can impersonate you, scam your friends, and even reset passwords to other accounts linked to your social media.
- Use a password manager to generate and store strong passwords.
- Never reuse passwords across different accounts.
- Enable Multi-Factor Authentication (MFA) to add an extra layer of protection.

2. Lock Down Your Privacy Settings

- Most social media platforms allow you to limit who can see your posts, contact you, or tag you in photos.
- Best privacy settings to enable:

Make your profile private – Only let approved followers see your posts.

Disable public tagging – Prevent others from tagging you in posts without your approval.

Limit who can send you friend requests/messages – Avoid unwanted contacts from scammers.

Turn off location tracking – Prevent apps from broadcasting your exact location.

- Tip: Periodically review your privacy settings on Facebook, Instagram, X (formerly Twitter), and LinkedIn to ensure your information is protected.

3. Be Wary of Suspicious Friend Requests and Messages

- Scammers and cybercriminals often create fake profiles to trick users into scams, phishing attempts, or impersonation fraud.
- Red flags of fake accounts:

Brand-new profile with very few posts or friends.

Random friend request from someone you don't know.

Suspicious messages claiming you won a contest or need to verify your account.

Requests for money, personal information, or login credentials.

- How to stay safe:

Only accept friend requests from people you know.

Never click on suspicious links sent via direct messages.

Report and block fake profiles immediately.

Managing Third-Party App Permissions

Be cautious with third-party apps that request access to your social media data. These apps—often quizzes, games, or tools—can harvest your information or even post on your behalf. Manage permissions regularly by reviewing app settings on platforms like Facebook or X (formerly Twitter) and revoking access where unnecessary. Limiting these connections reduces the risk of unintended data exposure.

Common Social Media Scams (and How to Avoid Them)

1. Phishing Scams

- Hackers send fake messages pretending to be from Facebook, Instagram, or X (formerly Twitter), asking you to "verify your account" or "reset your password."
- How to avoid it:

Always go directly to the official website instead of clicking on links in emails or messages.

Check for misspellings or unusual sender addresses.

2. Romance Scams

- Fraudsters create fake profiles, gain victims' trust, and pretend to be in love—only to eventually ask for money.
- How to avoid it:

Be skeptical of strangers who quickly profess love or urgency.

Never send money to someone you've never met in person.

3. "You Won a Prize" Scams

- A message claims you won a free iPhone, lottery, or giveaway, but you must pay a small "processing fee" to claim it.
- How to avoid it:

If you didn't enter a contest, you didn't win anything.

Never provide financial details to claim a "free prize."

4. Impersonation Scams

- Hackers clone a real person's profile (often a friend or family member) and message people pretending to need urgent financial help.
- How to avoid it:

If a "friend" asks for money, call them directly to confirm it's really them.

Report fake profiles immediately to prevent others from falling victim.

Social Media and Job Scams: LinkedIn Fraud

Professional networking sites like LinkedIn are also exploited by cybercriminals. Fake recruiters and job offers can trick users into providing personal data, banking details, or login credentials.

Common LinkedIn scams:

- Fake job offers requiring "security deposits."
- Requests for Social Security numbers, passport copies, or banking info.
- Unsolicited messages claiming you won a "business grant."

How to stay safe on LinkedIn:

- Only accept connections from verified professionals.
- Be cautious of too-good-to-be-true job offers from unknown companies.
- Never provide sensitive information before verifying a recruiter's legitimacy.

Final Thoughts on Social Media Privacy and Security

Think before you post – Oversharing can put you at risk. Enable strong security settings – Limit what strangers can see. Avoid common social media scams – Stay alert to phishing, fake profiles, and financial fraud. Use Multi-Factor Authentication (MFA) – Prevent hackers from accessing your accounts. Manage third-party app permissions to keep your data in check. By being smart, selective, and cautious, you can enjoy social media without compromising your privacy or security.

Chapter 8: Public Wi-Fi and VPNs – Staying Secure on Untrusted Networks

Public Wi-Fi is everywhere—coffee shops, airports, hotels, libraries, and even on public transportation. While it's convenient, it's also one of the riskiest ways to connect to the internet.

Hackers often target public Wi-Fi networks to steal personal information, intercept communications, and launch cyberattacks. Using an unsecured Wi-Fi network without protection is like shouting your private information across a crowded room.

In this chapter, you'll learn the dangers of public Wi-Fi, how hackers exploit unsecured networks, and how to protect yourself with VPNs and best practices.

The Dangers of Public Wi-Fi

Most public Wi-Fi networks lack encryption, meaning anyone on the same network can potentially see what you're doing. Cybercriminals take advantage of this in several ways:

- Man-in-the-Middle Attacks (MITM): Hackers secretly intercept data between your device and the internet, allowing them to steal passwords, credit card details, and personal messages.
- Rogue Hotspots (Evil Twin Attacks): A hacker creates a fake Wi-Fi network that looks like the real one. When you connect, they can monitor everything you do online.
- Packet Sniffing: Cybercriminals use tools to capture and analyze data being transmitted over an unsecured network.

- Malware Injection: If the network is compromised, hackers can send malware to your device through pop-ups or forced downloads.

Example: You're at a coffee shop and connect to "FreeCafeWiFi," assuming it's the official network. Unbeknownst to you, a hacker set up that Wi-Fi hotspot, and now they can see everything you type and access your personal accounts.

How to Stay Safe on Public Wi-Fi

1. Never Access Sensitive Accounts on Public Wi-Fi

- Avoid logging into bank accounts, email, or online shopping sites while connected to public Wi-Fi.
- Never enter credit card details or passwords on an unsecured network.
- If you must use public Wi-Fi for sensitive browsing, use a VPN!

2. Always Verify the Network Before Connecting

- Ask an employee for the official Wi-Fi network name before connecting.
- Beware of Wi-Fi networks with generic names like "Free Wi-Fi" — these could be rogue hotspots.
- If you accidentally connect to a hacker's Wi-Fi, they can steal your login credentials and personal data in seconds!

3. Disable Auto-Connect for Wi-Fi Networks

- Many devices automatically connect to previously joined networks, which can be dangerous if an attacker sets up a fake network with the same name.
- Go to your Wi-Fi settings and turn off auto-connect for public networks.
- Only manually join trusted networks.

4. Turn Off File Sharing and Bluetooth

- Public networks make your device more vulnerable to unauthorized access.
- Disable file sharing, AirDrop, and Bluetooth when using public Wi-Fi.
- On Windows and macOS, set your network type to "Public" to let your computer know it's on an untrusted network. This prevents it from automatically sharing files or being discoverable to other devices.

5. Use a VPN for Secure Browsing

- A Virtual Private Network (VPN) is the best way to protect yourself when using public Wi-Fi.
- How a VPN Works:

A VPN encrypts your internet traffic and routes it through a secure server, making it invisible to hackers, your internet provider, and even the government.

- Benefits of Using a VPN:

Prevents hackers from intercepting your data on public Wi-Fi.

Hides your IP address, making it harder for websites and advertisers to track you.

Allows secure access to content when traveling abroad (e.g., watching U.S. Netflix from Europe).

- Recommended VPNs: NordVPN, ExpressVPN, and ProtonVPN.
- If you frequently use public Wi-Fi, a VPN is a must-have.

Free VPN Options

For those on a budget, free VPN services like ProtonVPN's free tier are available. However, be aware that free VPNs often come with limitations in speed, data, and security features. They may also rely on ads or less robust encryption, so use them cautiously and consider upgrading to a paid plan for better protection.

Using Your Mobile Hotspot Instead of Public Wi-Fi

If you don't have a VPN and need a secure internet connection, use your phone's mobile hotspot instead of public Wi-Fi.

Why a mobile hotspot is safer:

- It creates a private, encrypted internet connection.
- Hackers can't intercept your data like they can on public Wi-Fi.
- It's a great backup option when you need secure browsing.

Tip: Set a strong password for your hotspot so strangers can't connect to it.

What to Do If You Think You've Been Hacked on Public Wi-Fi

1. Disconnect Immediately

- If something seems off (e.g., slow speeds, odd pop-ups, or login issues), turn off Wi-Fi right away.

2. Change Your Passwords

- If you logged into sensitive accounts while on public Wi-Fi, update your passwords immediately.

3. Scan for Malware

- Run an antivirus or anti-malware scan to check for infections.

4. Enable Multi-Factor Authentication (MFA)

- This adds an extra layer of security, making it harder for hackers to access your accounts.

Final Thoughts on Public Wi-Fi and VPN Security

Avoid using public Wi-Fi for sensitive transactions – If you must, use a VPN. Always verify Wi-Fi networks before connecting – Beware of rogue hotspots. Disable auto-connect, file sharing, and Bluetooth – Reduce exposure to hackers. Use a mobile hotspot or VPN – Both offer more security than public Wi-Fi. Free VPNs can be a budget-friendly option, but weigh their limitations carefully. By following these steps, you can stay safe while using the internet on the go without exposing your private data to hackers.

Chapter 9: What to Do if You Get Hacked

No matter how careful you are, no one is 100% immune to hacking. Even the most secure individuals and businesses can fall victim to cyberattacks, data breaches, or identity theft.

The key to minimizing damage is acting quickly and methodically. In this chapter, we'll cover the immediate steps to take if your accounts are compromised, how to regain control, and how to prevent future attacks.

Recognizing the Signs That You've Been Hacked

Sometimes, hacking is obvious—you get locked out of your accounts, or you see unauthorized transactions on your bank statement. Other times, the signs are more subtle.

Red Flags That Indicate You've Been Hacked:

- Unexpected Password Reset Emails – You receive password reset requests that you didn't initiate.
- Unusual Login Activity – Your account shows logins from unfamiliar locations or devices.
- Unauthorized Transactions – Strange charges appear on your bank or credit card statements.
- Friends Receive Suspicious Messages from You – Hackers may send phishing messages using your account.
- Sudden Changes to Account Settings – Your email, phone number, or security settings have been altered.
- You Can't Log In – Your password no longer works, and recovery options have been changed.

If you notice any of these warning signs, act immediately! The longer a hacker has access, the more damage they can do.

Immediate Steps to Take If You've Been Hacked

Step 1: Change Your Passwords Immediately

- If you still have access to your account, change your password immediately to prevent further damage.
- How to create a secure replacement password:

Use at least 12-16 characters with a mix of letters, numbers, and symbols.

DO NOT reuse old passwords—hackers may still have access.

Use a password manager (1Password, ProtonPass) to generate strong passwords.

- If you've lost access to your account, proceed to Step 2.

Step 2: Secure Your Email First

- Your email account is the gateway to everything—hackers can use it to reset passwords to other accounts.
- Steps to recover and secure your email:

Use the "Forgot Password" feature to reset your email password ASAP.

Enable Multi-Factor Authentication (MFA) to prevent future unauthorized logins.

Check and remove any unfamiliar recovery emails or phone numbers that may have been added by the hacker.

- If your email is compromised, it's critical to regain control ASAP!

Step 3: Check for Unauthorized Activity

- Bank and Credit Card Transactions – Look for unauthorized purchases and report them immediately.
- Social Media Accounts – Check for suspicious posts, messages, or friend requests.
- Emails Sent from Your Account – Hackers may have sent phishing emails using your identity.
- Cloud Storage (Google Drive, iCloud, Dropbox) – Ensure no sensitive files have been stolen or altered.

Step 4: Log Out Hackers from Your Accounts

- Many online services allow you to log out all active sessions remotely.
- How to sign out hackers from your accounts:

Google: Go to Security > Manage Devices > Sign Out of All Devices.

Facebook: Navigate to Settings > Security > Where You're Logged In.

Banking Apps: Contact customer support if suspicious logins occur.

Step 5: Scan Your Devices for Malware

- If a hacker gained access to your account, they may have installed malware on your computer or phone.
- Run a Full Security Scan:

Use Malwarebytes or Windows Defender to check for malicious software.

Update your operating system and apps—outdated software has security holes.

Remove any unfamiliar browser extensions that may be tracking your activity.

- If you find malware, disconnect from the internet and reset your device!

Quick Reference Checklist

- Consider this checklist for immediate action if you're hacked:
- Change all affected passwords.
- Secure your email with MFA.
- Check accounts for unauthorized activity.
- Log out hackers from all sessions.
- Scan devices for malware and remove threats.

What to Do If Your Financial Accounts Were Hacked

1. Contact Your Bank Immediately

- Report unauthorized charges or suspicious activity to your bank or credit card issuer.
- Freeze or replace compromised cards before more damage is done.

2. Report the Fraud to the Authorities

- In the U.S., report fraud to the FTC via identitytheft.gov.
- In the EU, report fraud to your local data protection authority.

3. Freeze Your Credit (Best Practice!)

- Cybercriminals steal identities to open fraudulent credit accounts.
- How to Freeze Your Credit:

Contact Experian, Equifax, and TransUnion to freeze your credit.

A credit freeze is free and prevents anyone from opening accounts in your name.

- Use a credit monitoring service to receive alerts about suspicious activity.

How to Prevent Future Hacks

- Enable Multi-Factor Authentication (MFA)

Use authenticator apps (Google Authenticator, Authy) instead of SMS-based MFA.

Turn on MFA for email, banking, and social media accounts.

- Use a Password Manager

1Password or ProtonPass can generate and store secure passwords.

Avoid reusing passwords—every account should have a unique password.

- Regularly Check for Data Breaches

Visit HaveIBeenPwned.com to see if your email or passwords have been leaked.

If your info is compromised, change your passwords immediately.

- Be Skeptical of Phishing Attempts

Never click suspicious links in emails or texts.

Verify requests from banks, friends, and companies by contacting them directly.

- Keep Your Devices Secure

Update your software and apps regularly to fix security vulnerabilities.

Use antivirus and anti-malware tools to prevent infections.

Final Thoughts: Recovering from a Hack

Stay calm – Quick action can mitigate the damage. Change your passwords and enable MFA to lock out hackers. Monitor your financial statements and report any fraud immediately. Freeze your credit to prevent identity theft. Use the checklist provided to streamline your response. Learn from the experience and enhance your security habits. By following these steps, you can minimize the damage from a cyberattack and strengthen your defenses against future hacks.

Conclusion: Your Digital Security Blueprint

Congratulations! You've taken a major step toward securing your digital life by learning how to protect yourself from cyber threats, scams, and hackers. The internet is a powerful tool, but with the right precautions, you can navigate it safely and confidently.

Key Takeaways from This Book

- **Passwords Are Your First Line of Defense:**

Use long, complex, and unique passwords for every account. A password manager can simplify this process.

- **Multi-Factor Authentication (MFA) Is a Must:**

Enable MFA on all important accounts (email, banking, social media) to add an extra layer of security.

- **Safe Browsing Habits Reduce Risk:**

Avoid clicking on suspicious links, phishing emails, or fake websites.

- **Your Devices Need Protection Too:**

Keep your operating system, apps, and antivirus software updated to prevent malware infections.

- **Financial Security Is Critical:**

Use secure payment methods, monitor transactions, and freeze your credit if necessary.

- **Social Media Can Be a Threat:**

Limit the personal information you share and adjust your privacy settings.

- **Public Wi-Fi Is a Hacker's Playground:**

Always use a VPN or mobile hotspot instead of unsecured public networks.

- **If You Get Hacked, Act Fast:**

Change your passwords, secure your email, scan for malware, and report any fraudulent activity immediately.

Building a Long-Term Cybersecurity Mindset

- Cybersecurity is an ongoing process. Here's how to stay ahead:
- Stay Informed: Follow trusted cybersecurity news sources to keep up with the latest threats and defenses. Regularly check for updates from reliable outlets to ensure your knowledge remains current.
- Use Security Tools: Keep your antivirus, VPN, and password manager updated.
- Think Before You Click: Be cautious with emails, messages, and websites.
- Regularly Review Your Security: Periodically update passwords and security settings.
- Help Others Stay Safe: Share your knowledge with friends and family to create a more secure digital community.

For visual learners, consider seeking out diagrams or infographics online to better understand complex concepts like VPN encryption or phishing attack flows. These can reinforce the strategies outlined here.

Final Thoughts

Online threats will always exist, but you now have the tools and knowledge to protect yourself. You don't have to be a cybersecurity expert—just follow good habits and use the right tools.

Now that you're armed with this digital security blueprint, go forth with confidence and stay protected.

Stay secure. Stay informed. Stay protected.

References

- Cybersecurity For Me. (2025). "Walmart Spark Driver Data Breach."

- Dark Reading. (2023). "T-Mobile Data Breach Affects 37 Million Customers."

- Qohash. (2024). "Ticketmaster Breach: 560 Million Customers Affected."

- Security Magazine. (2023). "T-Mobile May 2023 Breach Details."

- TIME. (2024). "Ticketmaster's Massive Data Breach Explained."

www.ingramcontent.com/pod-product-compliance
Lightning Source LLC
Chambersburg PA
CBHW071032050326
40689CB00014B/3616